TO A DIFFERENT DRUMMER

HELPING CHILDREN WITH LEARNING DISABILITIES

Mary Ann Dockstader, M.A.
Laurene Payne, B.A.

Published by

I.S.S. PUBLICATIONS
Instructional Support Services
160 Washington S.E., Suite 64
Albuquerque, New Mexico 87108
505/255-2872

Illustrations, book and cover design by Jamie Treat
Typography by Prototype

Printed in the United States of America
First printing

ISBN 0-915817-17-9

DEDICATION

We wish to thank our colleagues who contributed suggestions in the preparation of this book. Special thanks to Dr. Pat Sheffer, School Psychologist, for her critical evaluation. Particular gratitude is expressed to our families for their patience, understanding, and encouragement during the writing of this book.

This book is dedicated to learning disabled students everywhere, to their parents and teachers.

ACKNOWLEDGMENT

Our major thanks go to the following researchers and writers who have influenced our overall understanding of learning disabilities: Kephart, Kirk, Lerner, Slingerland, Johnson, and Myklebust. We have applied our understanding of their basic philosophy on learning problems in writing this book. Much of the information and remedial suggestions presented here have been accumulated over the years from experiences working in the diagnostic lab and in the classroom setting.

CONTENTS

Preface... 9
Introduction 11

PART ONE: Learning Disabilities and Your Child...... 13

Chapter 1: Children With Learning Disabilities:
                Who Are They? 17
Chapter 2: Causes Of Learning Disabilities 21
Chapter 3: Recognizing General Characteristics
                Of The Learning Disabled Child 29
Chapter 4: Confirming Your Child's Learning Disability.......... 37
Chapter 5: Your Feelings And Reactions 45

PART TWO: Remediation 49

Chapter 6: The Early Years.................................. 53
Chapter 7: The Middle Years 65
Chapter 8: Coping At Middle School 71
Chapter 9: Teen Years 79

PART THREE: Special Problems 85

Chapter 10: Attention Deficit Disorder 89
Chapter 11: Passive Behavior 93
Chapter 12: Aggressive Behavior 97
Chapter 13: Support Systems For Parents 103

Glossary 105
References 107

PREFACE

Every parent of a child with learning problems asks the question, "What can I do to help my child?" It is not an easy question for either parents or teachers to answer. Each child's needs are different and each parent's ability to help is different. At the same time, it is not possible for a teacher, at a particular moment, to remember all the activities that may be helpful or to find the time to describe what can be done. Teachers often resort to vague, poorly defined or impractical suggestions. This is a major source of frustation to parents and of very little help to children.

This book remedies the problem of inadequate information, advice, and suggestions. It provides parents and teachers with practical ways to help children who have learning problems. It is designed to bring understanding to those who seek information and to provide suggestions to those who seek to help. The content is neither academic nor clinical; rather, it is an overview of information about learning disabilities and includes many suggestions about resources and activities that can be extremely helpful to parents.

The earlier a learning problem is identified the earlier help can be given. The authors describe the common characteristics of learning disabilities in order to help parents and teachers identify ordinary developmental variations from more persistent and pervasive problems. Early assistance is needed to break the pattern of failure experienced by the child with learning disabilities. Frequent failure can produce low self-esteem and poor attitudes toward school. These feeling are hard to overcome once they are firmly established. Effective assistance is the antidote to failure.

The activities in this book are particularly engaging because each is a good learning experience and useful for all children. This means that the child with learning problems need not feel that he or she has been singled out for some unusual treatment. The majority of the activities have been selected from among those used with ordinary children and are included because of their particular usefulness to children with learning difficulties.

There are several secrets for success in helping the child or youth who has a learning disability. Activities need to engage the child in motivating and successful behavior. Activities need to be related to the specific needs of the child. Actions need to be appropriate to the age and grade level of the child or youth. In order to address these needs the authors cluster their suggestions around age groups. Suggestions include advice about how to approach the school, community resources, and specific teaching activities. The focus is on creating a successful relationship between home and school and on improving the child's chances for success in school.

This book is a major resource and reference guide for both parents and teachers who live and work with learning disabled children and youth. It recognizes that with a little information and help parents can provide significant assistance to their child. Teachers, with this guide, can assist parents with the practical suggestions and advice.

Gil Guerin, Ph.D.
San Jose State University

INTRODUCTION

Is your youngster having trouble in school as well as at home? Does he or she appear to be inattentive or overattentive? Forgetful? Does he appear to be stuck in the same behaviors? Are you suspicious that there might be a learning problem? Perhaps the teacher has told you that the problem might be a "learning disability." Are you confused by what that really means?

If so, you are not alone. All too often, parents become frustrated, angry, confused, and don't understand what is happening with their child, at home or at school. Nor do they know how to fully cope with the situation. If you find yourself in this situation, you have probably wondered how you can help a child who is unhappily failing in school because of a learning problem?

Welcome to *To A Different Drummer: Helping Children With Learning Disabilities*, a broad overview of what learning disabilities are all about. In addition to describing symptoms, patterns, and characteristics of learning disabilities, the book also offers concrete and practical suggestions to deal with everyday problems that special children face at home and at school. Many of the ideas and suggestions here have come from years of experience in the classroom setting and from talking with other consultants and colleagues in the educational field.

This easy-to-read handbook contains concrete and practical information on and explanations of learning disabilities. In incorporates examples, insights, ideas, and suggestions that have come out of classroom courses, workshops, and years of practical everyday remediations in the classroom. Designed to be used by parents with their children at home, our handbook can also be used by teachers as a resource in enhancing their own classroom program as they prepare to teach learning disabled children.

Mary Ann Dockstader, M.A.
and Laurene Payne, B.A.

PART ONE:

Learning Disabilities and Your Child

The chapters in this section will describe learning disabilities, their causes and characteristics. In many instances, we have included some case histories based on actual observations of children we have worked with. The chapters will also explore ways parents can begin to take action if they suspect their child has a learning problem—preliminary action at home as well as initial communication with the school their child attends. The closing chapter in this section will explore the feelings of learning disabled children and their parents once a diagnosis has confirmed that a learning problem exists.

CHAPTER 1

Children With Learning Disabilities: Who Are They?

Johnny is smart. The school tests prove it. He has the ability to do his classwork and the tests show that, too. And sometimes Johnny does fine in some subject areas, according to his teachers and his report card.

But for the most part Johnny is having a hard time learning things at home and at school. It's not because he can't learn or because he's listless, bewildered, disinterested, or stupid. Nor is this problem the result of ineffective teaching techniques, poor parenting, or the child's lack of motivation. Johnny probably has a genuine learning problem.

In learning disabled children, learning problems are caused by the inability to accurately perceive, interpret, or express what is seen and/or heard. These problems can interrupt the natural flow of learning to read, write, and do arithmetic.

Haven't you ever heard someone comment that, because Johnny is failing in school, he could do better if he "tried just a little harder," or "just worked a little longer"? Or how about . . .

    . . . "Boy, is she clumsy. She can't catch a ball!"
    . . . "He's always moving. I just can't keep him in his seat."
    . . . "She can't seem to listen. She never pays attention. She's never on task."
    . . . "He's a loner. He doesn't have any friends at school."

. . . "Why can't he stop talking for just five minutes?"

. . . "He knows his multiplication facts when he goes home, but he doesn't remember them the next day. Even tutoring doesn't help."

. . . "Why won't he behave in school?"

. . . "He's too young or immature for my class."

. . . "He's so good—tries so hard. Why can't he learn?"

. . . "He doesn't recognize any words, even after seeing them."

. . . "He still confuses letters that look similar."

. . . "He could not repeat a series of three words or numbers accurately."

. . . "She is always interrupting."

So what's wrong with a youngster who can't conform to the demands of his environment? He's probably learning disabled. Although a youngster may be alert, motivated, and eager to learn, he may find schoolwork hard to do and understand. A student who has trouble learning can have specific problems with reading, writing, or arithmetic. He is also generally unable to follow simple directions or remember his assignments. He may feel funny, different, or actually embarrassed because he can't tell time, understand basic measurements, or distinguish his left hand from his right, like other kids can do so easily.

Although learning disabled students want to learn, they sometimes become easily distracted or irritated at the slightest noise or movement

around them in the academic or home environment. Understanding simple oral directions or concentrating for short periods of time are difficult tasks for some of these kids to perform. Many of them tire easily, particularly when faced with repetitive tasks, such as learning math facts or cursive writing. Others become tense, anxious, depressed, or angry as a result of their frustrating school experience.

"Learning disabilities" is a general term which is used by schools in order to describe a variety of ways that individuals behave and learn. The problems may be most noticeable in sports, music, listening, conversing, organization, or many other life activities. In those areas, a child may feel weak and unsure, or be unable to perform at all.

Having a learning disability keeps a person from reaching his full potential. At that point, the person with a disability and the people around him become particularly frustrated. We know that the individual is extremely capable in some ways; why can't he just learn in school?

The term "learning disabilities," LD for short, was created to define a group of individuals whose learning process is stuck for some reason. Although estimates vary, some experts say that nearly two million school-age children are affected. These children, of average to above average intelligence, come from all economic levels and racial and ethnic backgrounds, and have no noticeable physical handicaps. These children short-circuit through their ears and eyes when it comes to learning language, spelling, calculations, sports, or judging space and time.

LD kids hear, see, taste, touch, and feel as well as any other child, but somewhere in their nervous systems LD kids have problems accurately receiving, processing, and expressing sensory information. Thus, they may display inappropriate behavior at home or at school. Although their intellectual potential is at one level, LD children function at a lower level. This is what identifies these children as learning disabled.

In 1968 the National Advisory Committee on Handicapped Children came out with the most widely cited and accepted definition of learning disabilities:

Children with specific learning disabilities exhibit a disorder in one or more of the basic psychological processes involved in understanding or in using spoken or written language. These may be manifested in disorders of listening, thinking, talking, reading, writing, spelling, or arithmetic. They include conditions which have been referred to as perceptual handicaps, brain injury, minimal brain dysfunction, dyslexia, developmental aphasia, etc. They do not include learning problems which are due primarily to visual, hearing, or motor handicaps, to mental retardation, or to emotional deprivation.[1]

Although a child may have a learning problem, one thing is certain— he *can* be helped. Early detection is important so that programs, services, and remediations can begin to have an impact. Loving and understanding parents, assisted by skilled professionals, can work together to discover each child's strengths and weaknesses. With this support most of these children can succeed in school and at home, eventually becoming well-adjusted, independent, and productive adults in today's world. Together we can do it!

1. National Advisory Committee on Handicapped Children. Special Education for Handicapped Children. First Annual Report. U.S. Dept. of Health, Education, and Welfare. Washington, D.C., Jan. 31, 1968.

CHAPTER 2

Causes of Learning Disabilities

Learning disabilities are *not* the fault of the child, nor do they occur because the parents aren't caring or conscientious. There is no simple explanation or reason for a child's learning disabilities, however the following list describes some possible factors that may contribute to learning problems.

During Pregnancy:

- Poor maternal nutrition
- Incompatible RH blood factors
- Infectious diseases, viral diseases or influenza that can affect the fetus
- Ingestion of certain drugs, alcoholism
- Poisonous toxins in the blood (toxemia)

During Birth:

- Premature delivery
- Long or hard deliveries causing anoxia (not enough oxygen to or in the brain)
- The use of forceps to deliver a baby, causing intracranial pressure at the time of birth
- Rapid delivery exposing the infant too quickly to a new air pressure
- Dry birth (water broken prematurely)
- Birth involving a cord around the neck
- Birth involving a breech delivery
- Low birth weight

Lifetime Experiences:

- An injury to the head
- High fever at an early age
- Diseases (for example, meningitis or encephalitis)
- Lead poisoning
- Severe or prolonged nutritional deprivation
- Drug abuse
- Brain injuries (such as lesions which destroy nerve tissue)
- Oxygen deprivation (i.e., at birth)

Some families seem to have a history of learning problems.

Heredity (Genetic Patterns):

- According to some of our case studies, some families seem to have a history of learning problems (for example, grandparents, uncles, aunts, brothers who have had reading or arithmetic problems or who were poor spellers). Studies done in this area seem to indicate that boys are more genetically affected than girls.

Other causes that might combine to make learning difficult for so many children include:

Biochemical Factors:

- Dr. B. Feingold[2] has been investigating the chemical structure of foods and its effect on the human body. He believes that consumption of food additives, such as artificial flavorings or colorings, and a child's sensitivity to sugar, contributes to learning difficulties in school.

Neurological Irregularities:

- According to Doman (1966) and Delacato[3] (1967), learning disabilities can be the result of an incomplete or interrupted neurological organization in the child's nervous system. Since the child's neurological organization is not complete, difficulties in learning occur. From their theory, Doman and Delacato developed a technique which patterned new neurological sequences in which a team of adults manipulates the child's limbs to create patterns of rolling over, creeping, crawling, walking, etc. The validity of these techniques is still being researched and questioned.

Learning disabled children do well intellectually in some areas, poorly in others.

Most authorities agree that learning disabilities are *not* caused by:

Mental Retardation:

- Mentally retarded children are consistently slow intellectually. Their development is generally slow throughout their lifetimes. Their capacity to function independently in society can sometimes be very limited. *Learning disabled children*, however, do well intellectually in some areas, poorly in others. There is often a marked gap between their capabilities and performance in school. Their skills are not easily maintained. There is often an erratic pattern of progress (gain then regression). Their attention spans are short; they're easily distracted and often restless. They can eventually make normal or better academic progress with specialized help. Finally, they function much more independently in society than mentally retarded individuals.

Deficit In The Sense Organs:

- LD kids are not usually visually or auditorially impaired. They may need glasses or use a hearing aid but their difficulties in learning are not primarily caused by these physical deficits. The eyes and ears of LD children usually receive accurate impressions, but the brain can't translate the impressions correctly. A central nervous dysfunction connected to the organs contributes to a learning problem.

  When LD children have perceptual difficulties, they can be helped by perceptual training programs consisting of training for perceptual accuracy. These remedial activities have helped children to perceive their surroundings more adequately.

Primarily Emotionally Disturbed:

- Emotional disturbance is not considered a *primary* factor among the causes of learning disabilities in children. Learning difficulties do not occur because the children are troubled, undisciplined, unwanted, or unloved; however, their emotional problems often *result* from their repeated failures and frustrations during their learning experiences. Though they may be eager and motivated to learn, their fear of failure, or fear of competing with peers, or fear of growing up contribute to their anxiety and anger.

Environmental Circumstances:

- If a child is living in a sterile environment with few stimuli such as books, music, or human contact, he may be considered environmentally deprived.

LD children model behavior from their immediate surroundings, just like all children normally do. They take opportunities to practice talking, reading, social skills, being a member of a group, taking on responsibilities, etc. Yet even children from stimulating homes or environments may still have trouble speaking, reading, writing, or doing math, thus causing concern that the child may be learning disabled.

It's probably not worth agonizing over the exact cause of the learning disability in your child. There's no point in trying to label him or treat him as a category instead of the unique individual that he or she is. As a parent, your primary goal is recognizing the problem as soon as possible, pinpointing the disability problem area, and getting help for your child. Setting up an educational plan that is right for your youngster and helping to remediate is what's important! In beginning to deal with this issue, you can help your child to discover what a really neat person he is by helping him to recognize his own strengths and weaknesses and to expand his own interests. With your love, cooperation, patience, and understanding, you can help your youngster make it! But remember, all things will take time.

2. Feingold, Ben F., *Why Your Child Is Hyperactive*, New York: Random House, 1975.

3. Delacato, C.H., *Neurological Organization and Reading*, Springfield, Illinois: Charles C. Thomas, 1966.

CHAPTER 3

Recognizing General Characteristics of The Learning Disabled Child

As a parent, you may begin to notice symptoms of a learning disability that start to show up before the child reaches school age and continue to be evident during his school years. Several characteristics of learning disabilities are listed and described below. For each, we have included a sample case history based on actual observation of students with whom we have worked.

Hyperactivity is a sign of learning disabilities in some children.

Physical Signs:

- *Overactivity* (hyperactivity)
  The child is constantly engaged in motor activity such as restless tapping of objects, fingers, hands, or feet. He may exhibit random and purposeless movement. He is also easily distracted by noises, voices, sounds, and lights.

Bobby is a bright-eyed eight-year-old boy who is extremely curious about how objects work. He is constantly wandering about the classroom disrupting and touching everything: desks, chairs, paints, as well as other students. During listening tasks Bobby has difficulty focusing his attention on oral instructions. When called upon for an answer he often responds, "I don't know" or "I can't." His comments are generally inappropriate, because he seems to be tuning in and out, catching only parts of the lesson. Though he is usually the first one finished with writing activities, his work is careless and incomplete.

- *Underactivity* (hypoactivity—the opposite of hyperactivity)
  The child seems to do everything in slow motion (passive or withdrawn).

Gail simply cannot complete a page of math facts during class time. No amount of cajoling or threatening helps. Although she knows the facts, it takes her forever to finish her work. She often erases to the point of tearing her paper, and she frequently starts over. Everything she does is in slow motion. Gail seems unable to alter the way she does things. It seems she would rather repeat the way she normally does things than take a risk in learning new ways to overcome the problem for fear of failure. Her face shows the frustration she is feeling, but she is unable to put her feelings into words.

• *Poor Coordination*
The child is awkward or generally clumsy. He is also poor in sports activity; he has poor handwriting and drawing performance (indications of immature motor development).

> Eleven-year-old Scott is tall and lanky for his age and is always falling over his own two feet. He even has difficulty sitting in his chair. The fidgety behavior he exhibits gets him in trouble with the teacher. In a crowd, Scott pushes, shoves, and bumps others, lacking awareness of how much space his body takes up. On the playground, his lack of skill running and hitting and throwing a ball causes him embarrassment. Scott still doesn't know his right hand from his left.

• *Poor Speech Development*
The child exhibits delayed or slow development of speech articulation (slow and difficult-to-understand speech).

> Susie is a third grader in our district who has difficulty talking to her peers. She mispronounces many words and is teased by her classmates. She acts shy and refuses to participate in class discussions. Susie substitutes, omits, or distorts consonant sounds such as *s*, *l*, and *r*. Susie has one close friend in class who often speaks for her.

Note: In addition to the above characteristics, parents can watch their preschoolers for symptoms that may alert them to possible problems. For instance, LD children often learn to crawl late (after 10 months), walk late (after 18 months), and speak late (still struggling to say very simple sentences after 24 months).

Behavior Signs:

- *Short Attention Span*
The child is easily distracted by noise and visual stimulus. The child is often unable to concentrate on any given task for very long.

> Johnny's teacher says he can't pay attention in class. He appears to be working at a normal pace but loses interest quickly on most assignments. His body is stationary, yet his eyes become fixed, as though he were daydreaming. Sometimes his eyes wander, searching out visual stimulus. His teacher reports that she constantly has to call Johnny back on task. During listening tasks, Johnny focuses his attention to other sounds in the room rather than focusing on the teacher's voice.

- *Perseveration*
The child's attention becomes fixed upon a single task which is repeated over and over again (such as writing, copying, or verbal activity). This is a style in which a child hangs on to something he has heard, seen, or felt for an inordinate amount of time. Like a record that skips, he becomes stuck—unable to move forward with anything he is doing.

> Mark took 10 minutes of class time discussing the fact that someone called him a name on the playground.
>
> Kathy *knew* she had written the spelling word wrong. Yet on the second, third, fourth and fifth tries, she wrote it the same way.
>
> No one understood why Paul liked the sound of certain words and repeated them continually, over and over again—every day during lunch, recess, and PE. One of his favorite words was *Ralph*.

- *Excessive Moodiness*

The child's mood changes from hour to hour, from happiness to tantrums when angry. The child seems to misunderstand or misinterpret what he sees or hears.

Debbie's moods are unpredictable. One moment she is calm and working quietly. Within minutes her mood shifts drastically. She easily becomes upset or just overreacts emotionally even when someone asks her a question or glances her way. She often ends up yelling or crying, thus totally disrupting the classroom setting. Her easily hurt feelings then shift back to toughness. Her inconsistent display of emotions is like a powder keg. No one knows just when she will explode. It is almost as though Debbie has no blueprint to follow—no new way of understanding how she could be in control in changing her moods.

Children with learning disabilities sometimes have unpredictable shifts in mood.

- *Language Processing*

The child exhibits delayed or slow development of the understanding and use of spoken language. This child is unable to form phrases, clauses, or sentences which follow standard grammar.

George is a 10-year-old who has difficulty finding the words he needs to express himself. He frequently forgets such simple words as *pencil, paper, cat, table, neighbor,* and *toothbrush*. Since word retrieval is difficult for him, talking in complete sentences is even harder. He cannot initiate conversation or ask simple questions. Writing his thoughts on paper is impossible.

Note: Other behavioral signs to look for would be distractibility, disorganization, and immaturity, as evidenced by problems in the classroom with incomplete or inconsistent schoolwork, poor work organization, confused directions, and the inability to participate in class activities. The child could also have problems remembering letter sounds, math facts, simple directions, or the sequence of events. He may not copy well, struggling with printing or handwriting. Occasionally his eyes and ears misinterpret information. In themselves, none of these warning signs prove that a child has a learning disability. However, when such tendencies persist in a child who has a good vocabulary, average or superior intelligence, and an eagerness to learn, but who functions at a low level, it is then that a learning problem or disability could be present.

These case studies characterize a variety of ways in which learning disabilities can appear. These examples were provided to help you recognize some of the problems an LD child faces. The following chapter details specific patterns that frequently occur in the behavior of a learning disabled child as well as preliminary steps you can take to ensure that suspected problems are properly diagnosed.

CHAPTER 4

Confirming Your Child's Learning Disability

P arents can and need to observe their child to see what behavior patterns persist. During preschool years, children's mental (cognitive) and language skills are developing to help them sort, classify, and categorize all types of information. By the time youngsters reach school age, their readiness enables them to be formally educated in the public schools.

But a youngster with a learning disability may not have the readiness or the tools with which to learn. For this reason, early detection and remediation are especially important.

The lists that follow describe behaviors that may characterize a child with a learning disability. Please keep in mind that *most young children experience some of the following difficulties.* Don't worry over an isolated incident. However, suspect a learning problem if some or many of the following behavior patterns
  • *are persistent over a long period of time*, and
  • *interrupt normal growth and interactions to a marked degree.*

In Infancy (Birth to Three Years):

• Has trouble with sucking, nursing or digestion.
• Shows a dramatic delay in learning to talk, (still struggling to say very simple sentences after 24 months), sit, crawl (after 10 months),

or walk (after 18 months); or, totally skips the creeping/crawling stage, thus adding to noticeable motor problems in preschool years.
- Doesn't like to be held or cuddled.
- Has disturbed sleep patterns over prolonged periods of time.
- Has trouble tracking or following movements with the eyes as the child gets older.
- Over-reacts or responds excessively to sounds. Has lack of response to sounds that is not due to physical problems (i.e., ear infection, deafness).

In Preschool Years (Three to Five Years):

- Has difficulty receiving and repeating messages without getting them all mixed up (the language comes out jumbled or he starts and stops in the middle of a sentence or idea).
- Is easily distracted or pays attention to too many things all at once.
- Can't follow even the simplest of directions.
- Has poor eating habits or constantly desires to eat sugar (with no indication of a physical problem).
- Has disturbed sleep patterns over a long period of time.

- Cries excessively.
- Feels secure in the same seat or chair and refuses to change or even try new things.
- Can't make choices or choose alternatives; becomes anxious when structure or routine is changed.
- Lacks rhythm (uneven timing).
- Is unusually quiet or inactive, or very hyperactive.
- Has difficulty learning to run or skip.
- Has impulsive behavior; might do things that cause physical injury to himself or others.
- Lacks awareness of his own body within a space; tends to bump into people and things.
- Excessively avoids playing with other children.
- Exhibits repeated and excessive rocking motion.

In School Years:

- Exhibits social skills several years below his chronological age.
- Constantly seeks and craves recognition long after his preschool years are over.
- Still depends on adults to remind him of daily routine activities (e.g., shoe tying, chores, organizing things in his room).

A learning disabled child often still depends on adults to remind him of daily activities.

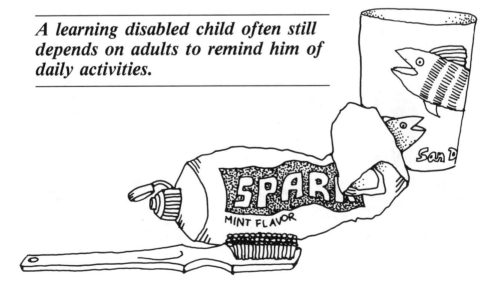

39

- Provokes trouble with other school or neighbor children or complains about being teased when, in fact, he is the center of attention (insecure, easily humiliated).
- Can't remember where to go (or gets lost frequently); loses his possessions often (e.g., toys, books, money).
- Gets lost in time and space; confuses up/down, in/out, over/under.
- Has a poor image of his own body (can't connect parts to a whole body).
- Would rather be thought of as dumb or stupid.
- Can't visualize or remember what he sees.
- Has a poor cursive handwriting or printing (poor hand-eye coordination).
- Constantly needs help with speech or retrieving vocabulary words; needs lots of help reading.
- Has problems buttoning, cutting, tying, coloring inside the lines; can't match shapes (circles, rectangles, etc.).
- At age eight, still reads *on* for *no*, *d* for *b*, has problems remembering the sequence of letters that make up a word (letters and words are confused or backwards), or can't build words from letters.
- At age eight, still writes *31* as *13*, or is unable to understand number concepts; has a problem counting.
- Can't draw shapes or copy letters.
- Has good verbal ability but has trouble reading (reading mechanically without comprehension).
- Has difficulty expressing ideas verbally or in writing.
- Has difficulty playing games and following the rules.

- Has difficulty with motor skills (hopping, running, skipping); awkward when it comes to body movement in sports (catching or batting a ball).
- Is an intelligent child (average to above average ability) who fails at school or whose schoolwork is erratic.
- Has difficulty distinguishing concepts of left/right.
- Is not learning; not wanting to go to school.
- Is disorganized.
- Is easily frustrated when doing academic tasks.
- Feels as though he can't keep up.
- Has uneven test scores, erratic daily performance.
- Lacks abstract reasoning and critical thinking skills.
- Lacks a sense of humor.

If many of these problems are frequent or severe, preventing the child from participating in class activities or completing homework consistently, then there may be cause for concern. Although the causes of learning disabilities may be vague or hard to understand, steps can be taken to help the child cope.

What Parents Can Do At Home

If, after observing your child to see what patterns persist, you are convinced that your child may have a learning problem, then *you* can take action:

- Consider arranging for a complete *physical examination* for the child. Talk to your pediatrician about your concerns. The doctor may find that allergies or diet may be contributing to the learning problem. Consider getting a good *visual examination* from a reliable optometrist. Have the child properly tested for *hearing accuracy.* Your doctor can probably recommend a good audiologist.
- Examine your own complete family history and write down details that include facts about pregnancy, birth disease, accidents, and patterned behavior problems. All of this information will aid specialists in diagnosing a possible learning problem.
- If you have a preschool-aged child, check with your local public school to see if programs are available locally in your area. Observe Jamboree

or classes given at the Y for kids or school-aged children.

- Begin investigating community resources. Find out what diagnostic clinics, tutoring centers, private and public schools, and public health agencies have to offer the child who might be learning disabled.
- Communication between home and school concerning the success of your child's education is very important. Discuss your concerns about your child's performance and learning difficulties with your child's teacher. She may give you suggestions on how to help your child and refer you to a specialist at school.
- Learn what your rights are by contacting the Office of Special Education, State Department of Education, or by calling your local school district office for more information.

Communication between home and school is very important.

- Talk to the school *principal, counselor,* or *school psychologist* about getting some special testing done. Become familiar with steps involved in getting a diagnostic battery or evaluation done on your child. Request testing if you feel there is a need (if you suspect a learning problem or disability).

- When testing is completed, meet with the *Child Study Team* at school. This group can consist of regular classroom teacher, Special Education teacher, psychologist, speech and language therapist, nurse, administrator, adaptive phys ed teacher, and counselor. Discuss your child's learning strengths and weaknesses. Become an active participating member in planning your child's education.
- Talk to a *physical education specialist* who can give you tips or suggestions on ways to improve your child's motor skills, body rhythm, and overall coordination.
- Talk with the *speech and language therapist* on ways to improve your child's vocabulary and communication skills.
- Sometimes the school personnel refer a parent to community organizations, such as Scouts, church organizations, community activities, or sporting leagues, to help improve the self-image of the learning disabled child. Encouraging a child to attend a social function or become involved with a hobby will also improve social skills.
- School professionals can familiarize you with the terminology used in dealing and living with a learning disabled child. Read books and other literature. Ask questions. Talk about your concerns and get the answers you are seeking. Contact your state and local chapters of associations regarding learning disabilities. Ask the school for the address of your nearest support group.
- Resist criticizing the child for mistakes made at home and school. Correct mistakes instead with the understanding that they are part of the learning process. Kids need to feel secure and they seek your approval. Their pace may be slow but the results of your patience and acceptance can be rewarding.

School districts, teachers, and parents agree that early intervention is essential if children with learning disabilities are to benefit significantly. Difficulties may be recognized at different points in a child's school career. Educational programs consisting of individualized and small group instructions, can provide an enjoyable and stimulating learning environment which aids the child's growth and development. Parents who support and reinforce a child's progress at home also contribute to the youngster's success.

So parents, if you suspect that your child may need special services, don't wait. Get involved and take advantage of your state and local resources. We commend those parents who are willing to participate as team members with school staff to work on ways to deal with the child whose learning pattern is different. As members of a team, we can find alternatives in helping him compensate for his disability. Although understanding the problem will take time, and the process and commitment will be ongoing, learning disabilities *can* be overcome to a greater extent today than ever before.

CHAPTER 5

Your Feelings and Reactions

O kay. So your perfectly normal-looking, intelligent child, who just doesn't learn as other children his age do, has been diagnosed as having a learning disability. Testing has confirmed parent and teacher suspicions. At this point, most parents seem to go through a gamut of feelings or emotional stages once they learn their child is learning disabled.

The first response for some is denial ("There's nothing wrong with him!" "She's really bright. She only needs more time to learn her assignments." "That teacher doesn't really understand my son, and doesn't know how to teach him." "All the problems will go away soon. He'll outgrow them because he's a good boy.").

Sometimes parents want to run or flee from the problem ("These professionals are wrong! I'm going to a different doctor, or a specialist." "Perhaps if we move!").

Others feel isolated ("So you told me he's different—do you really care?" "Doesn't anyone understand?"), or angry ("That psychologist doesn't really know my child." "I hate that teacher. She's not effective in the classroom with my daughter." "Why wasn't this problem diagnosed earlier?").

Then there are the feelings of guilt ("Why is this happening to my daughter? Is God punishing me?" "If only I had been a better parent!"), or blame ("It's the school's fault!" "It comes from your side of the family, dear." "Susie isn't trying hard enough—she's just lazy!").

Typical, too, is the feeling of fear ("Maybe it's worse than they say, or are willing to admit." "Will my child die?" "If he has a learning disability, will it prevent him from holding down a job, or from getting married?" "Will he ever finish school?" "What do I say when Freddy says he feels stupid?").

Parents often feel envy ("Everyone else's kids are lucky—everything comes easy for them." "As parents, we've tried our best. It's not fair!"). Parents may even sense a feeling of relief once someone confirms that their child has a learning problem.

You may be experiencing a lot of these same feelings. The range can be pretty overwhelming, producing secondary feelings of helplessness, confusion, and dismay. You may also be feeling stuck in dealing with these emotions. Eventually many of these initial feelings give way to acceptance and hope. Once you begin to recognize that there really is a problem and once you acknowledge how you really feel, then you can begin to help your youngster—to recognize his strengths and weaknesses, to talk to him honestly and openly about his learning problem and, with praise and encouragement, build his sense of self-worth. Whatever the feelings you experience, learning to accept, understand, and interact with a child who learns differently will be an ongoing process that will take time.

PART TWO:

Remediation

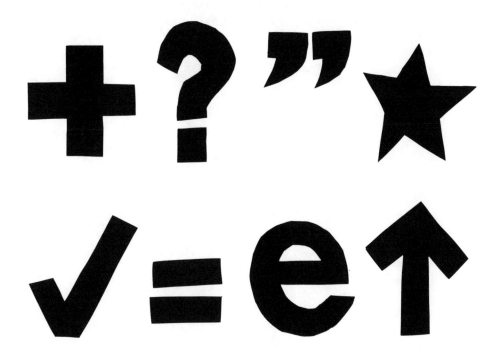

As a parent, you are a very important and influential person in your son's or daughter's life. In the following section, we present numerous suggestions on how you can help your learning disabled child at home. These activities include, at the earlier stages, body awareness, motor skills, vocabulary stimulation, and visual and auditory (listening) skills. Suggestions for older children include work with symbols, coping behavior, and organizational and self-management capabilities. All of the activities suggested are designed to help develop the basic skills necessary for learning in the LD child.

Although the remediations are listed for specific age groups—from preschool through college—you may wish to pick activities at which your child will experience success. Begin with easier activities and move to more challenging ones at the same or higher grade levels. Maintain contact with the school to coordinate your efforts and support the work they are doing. Even if your child is in mainstream classes, he or she can benefit from participating in the activities and working with you.

As you look over the lists in the following chapters, try to identify one or two activities to start with. We recognize the demands of working and trying to keep things going at home, particularly if you're a single parent. But we can't emphasize strongly enough the importance of practicing these activities to help your child develop and keep up with everyday schoolwork. As your remediation routine becomes established, extend the time you spend together as well as the number of activities you attempt. Helping to remediate not only can be fun, but can teach responsibility and independence that is needed for school and throughout life.

You *can* make a difference!

CHAPTER 6

The Early Years
(through Grade 3)

This chapter presents remediation activities for young children. The first set of activities is designed for preschool-aged youngsters; the second set is for children in grades 1 through 3. You may wish to get a family member or friend to help with some of the activities. In working with your child, keep the following in mind:

- Begin from where the child is now. Help him build and improve on what he already knows.
- Encourage and wait for eye contact before beginning any of the exercises.
- Use lots of repetition with each exercise.
- Choose a time you can be patient and caring.
- Encourage the child to do his best. Stay positive and generously praise his participation, performance, and efforts.
- Have fun!

Activities for Preschool-Aged Children

Motor Skills (Gross Motor)

Example:

"Annie can't roll the ball where she wants it to go. Nor can she grasp or hold on to her large toys."

Remediations:

- Help the child do stomach rolls.
  a. Child rolls up like a jelly roll in a sleeping bag or large towel. You press and roll slowly across the room.
  b. Child rolls himself across the room and targets his head to land in a certain spot.
- Have the child practice rolling, kicking, throwing, bouncing a ball.
- Have the child practice walking, skipping, running, jumping forward and backward, hopping.
- Have the child jump over boxes or cracks in the sidewalk.
- Practice balancing (on one foot).
- Ask the child to touch opposite toes (good for balancing and crossing midline).
- Have the child crawl over and under things. Use vocabulary to describe what the child is doing.
- Encourage the child to build, play with, or stack building blocks.

- Practice catching a ball in a bleach bottle with the bottom cut out.
- Toss a bean bag.
- Play hopscotch, tag.
- Dance.
- Have the child gallop, trot, march, clap to music.
- Swing.
- Climb on the jungle gym, playground equipment.
- Jump on a trampoline.

- Practice balancing (walking forward and backward on tiptoes), walking along a white line or on a 2″ × 4″ on the ground.
- Do a duck walk, rabbit hop, or elephant walk.
- Do somersaults.
- Practice moving body parts (moving the head or arms or legs in circles, beginning with small circles and then the circles get larger).
- Play hoop games (running or skipping beside a hoop or inner tube as it is rolling).
- Do simple obstacle runs, ladder walk (place ladder flat on ground, walk forward and backward between rungs).
- Play singing games ("Ring Around The Rosie," "This Is The Way We Wash Our Clothes," "Farmer In The Dell").
- Play pretend games (to be a bird in a tree, an elephant washing himself or cooling off, a cat catching a mouse, an alligator crossing a river, a rabbit hopping).
- Have the child play "ring toss" or drop objects into containers.
- Play "freeze" or "statue."
- Practice swimming activities or games in the water where the child uses both sides of his body (doggy paddle).
- Punch inflated toys that have a weight in the bottom of them.
- Use a scooter board (lying flat or sitting on a board to propel around cardboard boxes).
- Walk the wiggly line (follow the twisted pattern of a jump rope on the ground).
- Draw in the dirt (practice moving arm or stick across the entire body—left to right).
- Play "Simon Says"; point to body parts.
- Stand up, sit down with eyes opened and closed.

Motor Skills (Fine Motor)

Example:

> "Paula can't hold on to her crayon when she colors. She can't stack blocks or turn the knob on the TV set."

Remediations:

- Trace over lines, outlines, over numbers.
- Color.

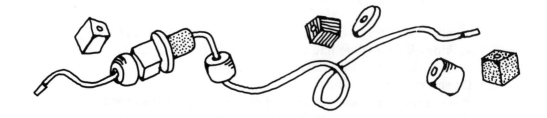

- Finger paint; do finger shadows, finger plays.
- Practice buttoning.
- Practice dressing oneself or dressing dolls.
- Practice lacing shoes.
- String beads.
- Cut with scissors.
- Trace numbers, letters, designs in wet or dry sand.
- Work with papier-mâché.
- Work with clay.
- Work puzzles.
- Use pegboards.
- Use dot-to-dot books.
- Paste string or felt on cardboard to make a picture or design.
- Sort buttons, keys, bottle tops.
- Play with construction toys such as Lincoln Logs, plastic building blocks that link or lock.
- Fold paper to make designs or objects (e.g., airplanes, animals).
- Play with toys that build small muscles (e.g., wooden and cardboard blocks, tempera paints and large brushes, plastic containers for water and sand).
- Play with toys that require the child to push, pull, zip, etc.
- Throw objects (balloons, yarn balls, wet sponges) at targets.
- Clip and unclip clothespins.
- Pour water into different sized cups.

Listening Skills

Example:

> "Charlie cannot follow simple instructions like 'Roll the ball to daddy.' He can't label the sounds in his surroundings."

Remediations:

- Play "Simon Says."
- Read to the child. Discuss the story. Ask him to predict what will come next. Share favorite parts or anecdotes.
- Have the child repeat what you say to him (for example, songs, riddles, rhymes). Repeat directions, numbers, or alphabet letters.
- Whisper to the child.
- Have the child identify sounds (for example, cat's meow, the noise a fire truck makes, water running, a dog's bark, sneezing, paper tearing, jingling money).
- Have the child "show me" (how the elephants walk or look).
- Have the child identify sounds or voices he hears or where he is when blindfolded.
- Instruct the child to move specific body parts on command (nod your head, clap your hands, stamp your feet, put head to floor, toes to wall, fingers to nose).
- Have the child point to objects you name.
- Encourage a "listening" posture (sitting on the floor, hands folded, eyes on the speaker).
- With the child's eyes closed, have him tell you how many times you clapped your hands or bounced the ball. If he doesn't know how to count, have him repeat it to you or after you, imitating you.

- Have the youngster tell you if sounds are loud or soft (for example, a church bell, smoke alarm going off, the ticking of a clock). Discuss the differences in types of sounds.
- Give short, concise, simple directions for the youngster to do something (for example, stand up, hop on one foot, sit down, close the door, put the pencil on the table). Begin with one direction and slowly increase the number as he gets older or more capable.
- Provide music, a simple rhyme or song to learn. Sing along with your child.
- Discuss TV programs that are seen together.
- Have the child march to a beat.

Note: Don't rush the child when doing these activities. Reduce his anxieties by waiting patiently for his response.

Vocabulary Development

Example:

> "Johnny kept telling the same story over and over, because his vocabulary was limited."

Remediations:

- Use story starters (begin a story, child adds to the story where parent leaves off).
- Talk about concepts for "bigger than," "smaller than," "up and down," "next to," "in front of, behind."
- Put things in categories (for example: things you eat, things that are blue, things you wear, things that are round, tools you use in a garden, things that are tiny, things that are soft).
- Play guessing games such as "what am I describing?"
- Describe people, objects, animals, shapes, colors.
- Teach the concepts of "high and low," "in between," "over and under."
- Play the game of guessing objects in a bag. Put a few familiar objects in a soft bag or pillowcase. The child must feel one object at a time, describe it, and try to identify it before pulling it out of the bag to see if he's right.
- Encourage the child to share his day with you (what he did at the school playground, at the zoo, or at a birthday party).

Encourage the child to share his day with you.

- Talk about familiar and unfamiliar noises or objects. Talk about what people are doing, things in a supermarket, different types of transportation, etc.
- Practice tongue twisters (Sally sells seashells by the seashore).
- Act out or tell a story.
- Have the child finish rhymes like "Hickory, Dickory, Doc. The mouse ran up the _____."
- Have the child tell a story to an adult as the adult writes it down. Then share the story with the child by reading it back. The child can draw pictures for the story.
- Play "telephone." Have a make-believe conversation while teaching phone courtesy at the same time.
- Give clear, specific verbal commands: "Find me a leaf, please." "Get the book off the shelf, please."

- Model new words in full sentences for the child. Give him praise when the child learns a new word or concept.
- Call some things by the right name, others by a wrong name, to see if the child can catch the error.
- Name and discuss items as you walk through the grocery store, department store, park, post office, gas station.
- Describe your actions to the child as you do things ("I am making the bed").
- Talk, talk, talk, and talk some more (your child needs verbal interaction), *and listen, too.*

Visual Activities

Example:

"Mark doesn't understand why he got tackled when he was just walking across the field. He didn't realize or 'see' that there was a football game in progress."

Remediations:

- Play the "Animal Rummy" card game.
- Play "Concentration."
- Line up objects (such as toys, fruit, etc.). Take one away. Play "what's missing?"
- Find objects that are certain shapes (for example, squares, circles, triangles).

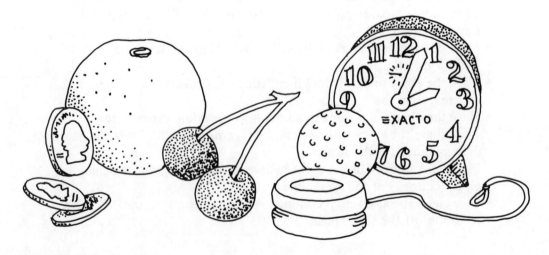

- Play with puzzles (simple jigsaw).
- Find and outline hidden shapes.
- Match designs, symbols, words. Find items that are not the same.
- Sort, categorize, classify different things such as animals, automobiles.
- Arrange objects (buttons, pans, pencils, match packs) in order, from darkest to lightest, smallest to largest, etc.
- Discuss directional landmarks.
- Practice with flash cards (for learning math or the alphabet).
- Take field trips around school or neighborhood and discuss observations. Draw pictures of what you saw.

Activities for Children in Grades 1–3

(Emphasis on Multi-Sensory Games,
Activities and Language Development)

Children with learning disabilities need to experience information in many different ways. This means that they benefit from using their eyes, ears, and sense of touch simultaneously when learning. This approach is called multi-sensory. Here are some multi-sensory remediations:

Speech and Language Development

- Practice tongue twisters.
- Ask specific and detailed questions. Request specific and detailed answers in return.
- Write down directions for the child to help him organize his day or chores.
- Play act with puppets to teach social behavior and to develop language.
- Label and talk about unfamiliar objects in the child's immediate environment.
- Play "20 Questions" or "I'm thinking of an animal with the first letter *k*."
- Involve the child regularly in conversation. Set aside specific times for sharing, listening, and asking questions.
- Verbalize the organization of tasks and steps in problem solving.
- Allow and encourage the child to verbalize his actions out loud while he works if it helps him concentrate.

Sensory Remediations

- Play "Morse Code" games (puzzles found in activity books which require the child to substitute letters for dots).
- Share reading experiences with your child. Discuss what you've read and what he has read today in school or at home.
- Read along with a record or tape (check your local library).
- Count with songs. Chant multiplication tables to the beat. Sing along with records or tapes; lip sync. Repeat and memorize lyrics to develop memory skills.
- Teach life skills at home (setting an alarm, learning how to use the phone).
- Make charts to show child's progress at home with chores, at school, in church.
- Begin collections of stamps, leaves, rocks, etc., to teach order of things (smallest to biggest), categorizing.
- Start photo albums, scrapbooks.
- Play cards and dominoes to help with math skills.
- Place salt in a box. Have the child use his index finger to trace letters, short words, or math facts in the salt (or trace on sandpaper).
- Use Scrabble letters to spell new words or study weekly spelling words.

Begin collections of stamps, leaves, or rocks to teach order and categorizing.

- Use a water squirt gun and/or paint brushes with water to practice math facts or spelling words on a sidewalk. Have the child squirt or draw with water the numbers (or words) as they are called out to him.
- Use shaving cream on the shower walls or a flashlight on a dark bedroom ceiling to "write out" spelling words or math facts.
- Provide pencil and paper activities such as coloring books, dot-to-dots, easy crosswords, word searches.
- Use flash cards (letters, numbers, math facts, spelling words).
- Use jump rope or string for writing out letters on the floor.
- Use chalk and chalkboard to practice handwriting, spelling or math, to draw geometric shapes, or just to play on while strengthening muscles.
- Begin teaching *very basic* concepts of time, such as hour and half-hour. Make a clock out of a paper plate to practice.
- Identify and handle coins. Play store.

CHAPTER 7

The Middle Years
(Grades 4–5)

The transition from 3rd to 4th grade is a time when students have to meet increasing academic demands. The emphasis shifts from learning how to write to using writing as a tool to express thoughts clearly on paper. Children are also expected to spend more time doing independent thinking tasks in the classroom around more complex ideas or processes. In addition, children encounter new and increasingly complex mathematical concepts. In Language Arts, students are expected to understand *more* of what they read, spell multi-syllable words, and write their ideas down in a more organized fashion.

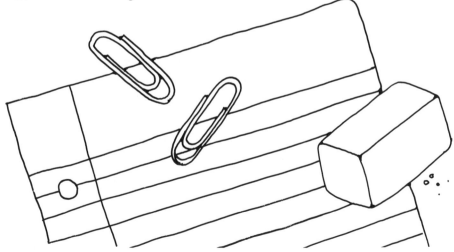

We recognize the fact that this transitional period is an anxious or stressful time for both child and parents. We strongly encourage parental involvement with the child's 4th grade teacher to become familiar with teaching styles, instructions, and expectations for that school year. You, as a parent, can then successfully reinforce the child at home. Here are some suggestions to assist you in remediation in the home environment.

Symbol Transition Remediation

- Make flash cards for recognition of cursive alphabet letters. Use them for sequencing of letters, sound blending, initial and ending sounds in words, review of vowels.
- Cut a sheet of white construction paper into 3″ × 4″ pieces. Write one vowel (*a, e, i, o,* or *u*) on each card; make several copies of each. Cut several sheets of orange construction paper into 3″ × 4″ cards, labeling each one with different consonant letters (one per card). Have the child trace the letter on the card with his finger, saying the name of the letter and the sound the letter makes. Use as flash cards for review.
- Use the same color-coded cards from the previous activity to spell out words. Have the child trace the word he spells out.
- If the child is still printing and continues to reverse *b*'s and *d*'s, *q*'s and *p*'s, *u*'s and *n*'s, choose *one* letter of the pair and have your son or daughter practice that letter over and over. For *b*'s and *d*'s discuss the "belly" of each. You can even make poster-size cutout letters for display.
- Cut out letters on sandpaper and have the child trace by touching them with a finger.
- Practice tracing cursive and manuscript letters over and over (use chalk, squirt gun on a sidewalk, flashlight on a dark bedroom ceiling). Provide a writing model for kids who are having problems with letter confusion, having them trace your correct *b*'s and *d*'s, *u*'s and *r*'s.
- Have the child use Scrabble letters or letters on cards to spell multi-syllable words you dictate.
- Continue to do motor activities (ping-pong, baseball, soccer) to reinforce and build coordination.
- Set aside time nightly (10–30 minutes) for family reading. (You will provide a valuable role model by using this time to read as well.)

Silent or oral reading every night (with no TV or radio) will increase a child's success in school.

- Parents and children can make up questions to ask each other after they have read something together. This task is particularly helpful if a child has an assignment that he needs help on. If the child is tired or bogged down by a lot of written homework, oral questions can help speed up comprehension of a particular assignment.
- Set aside a specific time for homework every night. A patterned routine should become established for completion of work. Use a timer if the child can't stay on task. The timer will aid him in completing his assignments. If necessary, set short breaks.
- Work on helping your child develop his vocabulary. Encourage him to write a daily diary about school activities, family field trips, church or club outings, everyday experiences.
- Help expand your child's interests by exposing him to children's magazines, books, games, social clubs, the local library, children's tapes and records. Encourage social experiences and outings that he may later write about in school.

Set aside a specific time for homework every night. A patterned routine should become established for completion of work.

- Limit the time your child watches television and offer your child choices within those limits. Encourage the family to watch educational programs together and discuss the programs either during or after the shows. Build on vocabulary. Ask the child *his* opinion and encourage him to ask questions. Listen to what he has to say.
- Whenever possible, go back to using concrete objects when teaching, reviewing, or reinforcing concepts (for example, oranges or counters to review addition or subtraction, or using and manipulating the hands on a wall clock to teach time).
- Play Yahtzee, Phonetic Lotto, card games such as "Concentration" (with pictures, letters or numbers), dominoes.
- Play rhyming or blending word games; use flash cards for memorizing multiplication tables.
- Encourage silent reading; ask questions about what he's read.
- Have your child write down something you dictate to him. Read what the child writes out loud to him so he can hear what he is writing.
- Have the child proofread what he writes before submitting the work to the teacher. Have him check for errors with your support, help, and encouragement. Proofreading may be very difficult for your child. It may help if he reads his work to you and you remind him to check for details such as capital letters and punctuation. Recognize the child's efforts and avoid criticism.
- Help your child to write down his ideas first before he tackles a long English or reading assignment. Then help edit for final copy.
- Help and encourage the student to use a Magic Marker to highlight difficult words in reading or underline spelling words to be memorized.
- Turn the child on to school supplies. Emphasize that a well-presented assignment (like a neatly prepared report in a good, clean folder) is preferable to a sloppy, torn paper or folder.
- Verbally brainstorm with your child before starting a writing assignment. Discuss and write down possible vocabulary words, main ideas, and themes. Discuss different story endings or beginnings. This will help generate ideas and structure.
- Have the child put due dates of academic assignments on a large calendar at home.
- Help your child meet deadlines by giving him reminders as to when

the project is due. Help him to set up a daily schedule for time to work on the assignment. The child may need you to structure his time at first so that he learns how to structure his own time in order to meet deadlines.

- Encourage the child to write down chores, appointments, or other expectations to consistently refer to. Because most children are visual learners, seeing the written words on paper, in a familiar spot in his room or in the kitchen, helps him learn and remember what is expected of him.
- Encourage and teach your child to use the dictionary at home, particularly on tough written assignments or on difficult spelling words. You can help by finding the right dictionary setting or page if necessary. Scan down the page together until you find the word.
- Help the child make scrapbooks. Help him write stories to go with the pictures.
- Increase everyday vocabulary by talking with your youngsters about words that mean the same or words that are opposite; play Password.
- Practice telling time using terms like "half past," "quarter of." Discuss the seasons. Practice, show, and use units of measurement (pounds, ounces, liters). Cook together to teach cooking skills and terminology. Count change.

Practice, show, and use mathematical measurements. Cook together to teach cooking skills and terminology.

- Take your child to the local library. Help him to find and use the card catalog, reference books, encyclopedia.
- Keep charts at home or achievement records to plot goals and progress the child makes. Praise and reward for goals achieved.
- Encourage your youngster to read aloud often; listen or take turns. If possible, ask comprehension questions prior to reading orally for better understanding.
- Buy "word search" or crossword puzzle books.
- Roll out dice that have letters on them to spell words. Play Scrabble, Vowel Lotto, or use anagrams to build words.
- Use a magnetic alphabet board to study and practice weekly spelling words.

For those children with learning problems, school-related tasks are extremely stressful and exhausting at this point in their lives. They are beginning to take more control of their own learning. Consequences and responsibilities are important things to be learned during this time. As parents, you need to be aware that your children need more rest, *structure*, and fun activities. More than ever make sure parental expectations are clear, realistic, and precise. Set goals and limits, but be careful and cautious not to overload your child.

CHAPTER 8

Coping at Middle School
(Grades 6–8)

Have you noticed that there are some dramatic changes taking place in your child lately? As in many 6th graders, physical, mental, and emotional changes are happening rapidly. Parents can't believe that this is the same "nice little Johnny or Susie" that existed just yesterday. These changes can affect diet, sleep, and even schoolwork.

During those preteen years self-identity becomes a big issue. Typically in the 6th, 7th, and 8th grades, students are generally not aware of the consequences for the choices they often make. If they have not experienced many of the outcomes, they will generally test to the limit at home, at school, and even in society to get the respect they want from classmates within the peer-pressuring structure.

By the 6th grade many children have become settled in learning styles and patterns. But, for a learning disabled child, weaknesses that existed throughout the school years could continue to interfere with future academic learning if the disability hasn't been totally remediated or corrected already. Because there are tremendous social pressures during these middle school years, the LD child will tend to hide his weak areas in order to appear normal to peers and even family members. He may even be at a greater loss in dealing with academics and even social popularity because he does not have the tools with which to cope, thus creating an extra burden for himself.

During the pre-teen years, self-identity becomes a big issue.

The remediations in this section offer ways in which the parent can help reinforce coping methods to ensure success for future academic progress and social interaction. While the activities in previous sections focused on *skills*, these suggestions are more oriented to self-management and overall achievement. It is most important that the child has a *good* knowledge of his own strengths and weaknesses so he can clearly communicate that to others. For example, if he can tell the teacher about his learning style or learning needs ("I can't remember oral directions," or "I have to write down all my assignments because I won't remember when I get home"), then the teacher has more information and can better serve him in the mainstream classroom.

With the tools we are about to suggest, he will begin to gain acceptance of himself and feel more comfortable in dealing with possible success and failure in the world around him, thus enabling him to make better personal decisions and take on more responsibility. It is therefore the responsibility of both the child and his parents to make a sincere and continuous effort to communicate with the school about the child's needs.

Building Student Coping Skills:

- Find out everything you can about the teacher's classroom (for example, grading system, homework policy, regular routine, availability of extra help). Help your child to understand the procedure.

- Direct the child back to his teacher if he has questions about the assignments or concepts taught in the lesson or in the classroom.
- When a child needs to ask for help from his teacher, have him practice asking questions by pretending you are the teacher. Model different ways of asking for help or assistance.
- Encourage your child to find a "buddy" in class who will help him take notes or answer questions about the assignment.
- Listen for possible problems or stresses in or about the classes. For example, does your child complain about
  - Not understanding his teacher(s)?
  - Not hearing the oral directions?
  - Not being able to copy down all the work from the board in the allotted time?
  - Not knowing what to study for a test?
- When problems arise in the class or failing grades appear, ask specific questions of the teacher and the student. Be creative about possible solutions. (For example: Would a daily homework assignment sheet be helpful? Would a weekly work contract, initialed by all teachers, help to improve the child's work?)
- Get a counselor involved. Have him help to discuss problems and explore solutions with the child, particularly if stress continues in the classroom.
- Negotiate schedules with your child for using the phone or watching television that will work for both you and your child.
- Help your child practice note taking from TV news reports.

- Be aware of long-term projects and book reports; help your child set daily and weekly goals toward project completion; use a calendar that can be seen easily.
- Use flash cards whenever possible to aid in learning. Use colored pens or pencils to emphasize vowels, letter blends, or word endings on flash cards.
- Practice patience.
- Ask the teacher if the student can use a tape recorder in class, especially when a long lecture is given.
- Share responsibilities for acquiring school supplies. Help the child develop independent skills by helping him shop, pay, and care for school supplies.

- Check with the teacher to see if your child needs to be on a workable *behavior* and *academic* contract where goals and expectations are clearly defined for the child.
- See if peer tutoring is available at the school.
- Help your child articulate effectively what his disabilities are so he can better communicate them to his teacher. (He should know by now that he has problems copying or that he reverses, for example.)
- Encourage your child to speak to the teacher privately about his strengths and weaknesses so he can achieve better in the classroom.
- If available, encourage your child to use a typewriter, computer, or word processor to assist him with an assignment.
- Check out library resources such as books with large printing, tapes to aid with library assignments, or novels on tapes.

- Give short and simple directions at home.
- Keep the home environment structured. Eliminate as many distractions as possible. Firm rules and routines are essential.
- Help your child define his responsibilities at home and at school.
- Look (and encourage your child to look) for groups of people who may share your child's interests. Encourage participation in scouts, church groups, and clubs.
- Always recognize positive behavior instead of drawing attention to negative behavior. Acknowledge genuine effort and student sincerity. Measure his ability, *not* his liability.
- Whether it be changing schools or changing environments, help your child make a smooth transition by visiting the new campus or neighborhood together. Talk to him about the changes—real and anticipated. Let him help you plan the move. Draw maps. Take practice runs to make the transition as smooth as possible.

Dealing With Teacher Expectation In Junior High:

During this period your child will need to adjust to the expectations of more than one teacher. It may take those teachers a while to get to know your child. Don't be surprised if you hear the following comments:

"I hate that teacher!"

"My history teacher yells at me for no reason!"

"My math teacher doesn't like me!"

"He gave me an F and I don't know why."

"The teacher gave us too much homework. I can't keep up with the class."

"I don't know what's going on in class. I don't know what's expected of me."

It's an all-too-familiar pattern. Because a learning disabled child often feels lost in dealing with his school environment, he often misses cues and has trouble adjusting or being flexible in different classroom situations. Coping with different mainstream teachers can be a frustrating experience. Here are a few suggestions for discovering what teachers expect in their classrooms:

When a child feels negative about a teacher, brainstorm ways to cope with or solve the problem.

- Take advantage of Back-To-School Night. Key in on what the teachers say and want as far as curriculum and behavior expectations are concerned.
- Familiarize yourself with the school's disciplinary policies. Help your child understand the rules and regulations.
- Ask your child direct questions about the day's activities at school. Listen to his or her feedback.
- If there really seems to be a problem, find out from the teacher what's bothering him about your child's behavior.
- Help your youngster find alternative ways in dealing with different teaching personalities and styles. Include other resources, such as his Special Education teacher, counselor, vice-principal, to assist.
- When a child comes home feeling negative about a teacher, make it a challenge by brainstorming to find ways which will help him to cope or to solve the problem. It is advisable for the parents not to take sides, especially against the teacher. Let the child decide how he will deal with the problem.

- Take advantage of parent–student–teacher conferences. Request a meeting if necessary—that is your right. Don't be afraid to request that a member of the Child-Study Team be present to help in planning to make it a more positive learning environment.
- Make weekly or monthly checks with the teacher(s) to see how progress is going.
- Encourage your child to seek after-school help from his mainstream (regular) teachers. You might be surprised how a teacher will respond in a positive manner once the teacher knows the LD child is motivated or willing to learn.
- Show your support and don't go into meetings or conferences in a negative manner. Pattern or model positiveness when dealing with the school.

Parents frequently see kids doing things that appear to be the result of defiance or willful rebellion when, in fact, the disability may be at the root of some of this behavior. In this way, the child's behavior patterns are often misunderstood by school personnel and parents as well. We strongly encourage you to look beyond the defiance and try to separate the disability from the anger. If Johnny doesn't clean his room when you tell him to and it makes you angry, is it because Johnny is defiant or is it because Johnny can't remember oral directions? Work it out. Help him to compensate. Give him ideas of how to help himself because acting out may be a way for Johnny to cope until he learns a better way to do things. Above all, remember: this, too, will pass.

CHAPTER 9

Teen Years
(Grade 9 through College)

As your child begins high school you are faced with a dilemma. At this time you may notice a growing independence and self-reliance in your child, but you may also be aware of his anxiety and insecurity. You would like to encourage his desire for more responsibility, but you might wonder about the choices he is making. Letting go of your expectations can be extremely difficult, and yet your teenager may need you more than ever.

High school can be a frightening experience for a person with learning disabilities. In regular classes, the workload is difficult and there are many students in the class. Your child has to assertively request assistance. Information may be delivered at a fast pace and assignments may be confusing. Academically, your child will have to draw on all his strengths in order to compensate and cope.

Like all individuals in high school, your child looks for his social place in the group. He or she may worry about acne, weight problems, menstruation, late or early development, sexual arousal, school pressures, boredom, parent hassles, peer pressure, and money problems. Pressures to become accepted may lead your child into drug involvement or other unacceptable activities. It is important that you continue to be consistent with your values and standards; don't be afraid to seek outside help through family counseling or support groups. It is true that your teenager now begins to make his own decisions, but he needs your help and experience to show him options.

As the child moves on to become the young adult, it is important to remember that the parent now becomes a consultant, counselor, and advocate instead of a caretaker. As your role shifts, keep in mind that it will take time for your teenager to adapt to the adult world. Here are some suggestions for helping him make his own decisions:

Career Goals/Life Skills:

- Talk to your teenager about his dreams, desires, and plans.
- Go to Open House and meet his teachers. Record what is expected by the teachers and discuss their expectations with your teenager.
- With your teenager, meet with the counselor and/or Special Education teacher to set up a viable schedule of classes.
- Find out what is required to achieve a high school diploma or meet graduation requirements.

- With your teenager, meet with his counselor or career counselor to gather information about vocational training, job opportunities, work-study programs and career choices. In some cases these programs can begin in high school.

Challenge your teenager to try new things and pursue outside interests.

- When your teenager talks to you, give him your full attention. Don't watch TV, read, or do other activities when he is speaking or addressing you.
- Share with your teenager the outside world of banking, grocery shopping, and budgeting. Help him learn how to make change, balance a checkbook, read bus destinations and schedules, read meters, fill out applications, write resumés, and pay bills.
- Encourage him to read the classified section of the newspaper, such as want ads for cars or apartments.
- Teach your child the organization of a newspaper.
- Give him practice in looking up phone numbers and making long-distance phone calls and appointments (hairdresser, doctor).
- Provide for driver's training. Help him read the driver's manual, giving extra explanation as needed.
- Designate more responsibilities around the house.
- Encourage him to pursue his outside interests, such as sports or clubs.

- Help refine social interactions; practice rules of etiquette.
- Encourage him to take on responsibilities outside the home, such as a part-time job, volunteer work, or community service.

Encourage responsibilities outside the home—a part-time job, for example.

- Help teenagers make up-to-date choices about clothing, hairstyles, and hygiene.
- Encourage him to join social organizations at school.
- Give extra encouragement and praise to reinforce a sense of accomplishment.
- Challenge your teenager to try new things.
- Encourage him to be as independent as possible.
- Have your teenager participate in family decisions.
- Allow your teenager to express his ideas, feelings, and opinions; avoid making judgments even if you do not agree.
- Use a courteous tone in your voice when communicating with your teenager.
- Take an interest in your teenager's activities.
- Try to not over-react.

The teenage years are an emotional roller coaster. It is a time when your teenager will want to be an adult one minute and a child the next. The person with learning disabilities will need a lot of extra support to learn ways to cope with external and internal pressures. It is a good idea to be consistent with rules, but view the mistakes that your teenager may make in light of the problem he has had.

Getting Ready For The Future:

Now that your child's high school education is drawing to a close, it is important to know that there are educational and vocational programs available. The Special Education counselor in the high school is a good source for information regarding four-year colleges, junior colleges, and vocational programs in your area. Once your child makes a decision about his future, ask the counselor to help coordinate college entrance testing procedures.

Note that entrance exams may be taken with assistance. For example, someone with reading problems may request a reader or permission to take the test orally. These services can be provided, but special arrangements need to be made *early* in the senior year.

In planning for college, consider that many colleges provide the following services: readers, tutors, special equipment, alternative test procedures, career counseling, support groups, and liaisons between the student and teacher or community.

It is important to realize that the high school LD graduate will continue to need some support and guidance, while becoming more self-reliant in the adult world. For he, too, wants to succeed.

84

PART THREE:
Special Problems

In the following three chapters, we discuss special behaviors that may be displayed by children with learning disabilities. Attention Deficit Disorder, Passive Behavior, or Aggressive Behavior, which may be symptomatic of learning disabilities, can cause the child a great deal of stress in the classroom. These behaviors interrupt the learning process and are not well-tolerated by many teachers. When these behaviors are displayed, they are so far from the norm that particular remediations are necessary.

The remediations included in these chapters are intended to make children aware of their behaviors as well as to give them a blueprint for more positive alternatives. Please note that none of these special behaviors are themselves learning disorders and that not all children who exhibit these behaviors are learning disabled. But since these behaviors are an additional burden for LD children who do exhibit them, these additional remediations are especially important.

Because the behaviors described in these chapters tend to elicit negative and sometimes extreme responses, a child with these special problems is extremely vulnerable to low self-esteem. With remediation, he will begin to behave more like the other students in the class. With an increase in social acceptability and a decrease in negative adult responses, his self-esteem begins to build.

Incorporate the behavioral remediation suggestions with previously mentioned skill-related ideas to help the learning disabled child succeed.

CHAPTER 10

Attention Deficit Disorders

Stephanie, now age seven, had been a concern to her parents and teachers for some time because of her highly visible behavior. She was considered to be overactive, inattentive, and moody. She seldom sat still. Even in preschool, Stephanie appeared to have problems getting along in a group setting. She couldn't sit down and color for more than a few minutes. Nor could she watch a whole Sesame Street program. As she grew older the behavior patterns continued. She had problems focusing her attention in the classroom, lacked the ability to follow school rules, had a poor self-image, lacked social skills, and was easily distracted by noise and other children in the classroom setting. She always seemed preoccupied.

Does your child have trouble paying attention? Does he seem to always be "on the go?" If so, he may be experiencing what is termed an Attention Deficit Disorder (or ADD).

ADD describes a combination of observable behaviors which can greatly impact a child's interaction with his surroundings. Perhaps he gets distracted easily, requires immediate rewards, or acts before thinking. He may seem to be constantly moving and chances are he is having problems interacting with others at home and at school. If he exhibits just some of these behaviors, social and academic problems can occur.

A child with Attention Deficit Disorder may not consider any consequences prior to acting.

A child with Attention Deficit Disorder may exhibit the following behaviors:

- *Cannot Pay Attention; Easily Distracted:*
  - Becomes distracted by sounds, lights, movement.
  - Cannot focus on what is important or ignore the unimportant.
  - Less able to focus and attend to a task than other children of his own age.
- *Acts Without Thinking First:*
  - Does not consider any consequences prior to acting.
  - Knows the rules but plans his actions poorly.
- *Has Trouble Accomplishing Long-Term Goals:*
  - Wants immediate feedback without *any* delay.
  - Requires frequent short successes to stay on task.
  - Without immediate praise, may leave work incomplete or abandon long-term goals.
- *Has Extremely High Energy Level:*
  - Is restless and overactive (hyperactive); may be too energetic for the activity (can't sit through a 30-minute cartoon show).
  - Has difficulty functioning in quiet environments (can't sit still in church).
  - Exhibits intense emotions inappropriate for his age.

Remediations for ADD: (Ages 5 and up)

- Provide structure and consistency to daily routines and schedules.
- Define rules clearly.
- Make expectations and consequences clear and concise without negative emotions.
- Heap on encouragement and praise often as these kids are easily discouraged. Don't humiliate them.
- Show warm, loving affection often.
- Give them opportunities and responsibilities in which they *can* succeed.
- Structure a quiet place for the child to do academic work (homework).
- Break down chores and tasks to simple step procedures.
- Try to keep the environment quiet and calm with one activity at a time.
- Avoid poorly supervised parties or unstructured play time.
- Reduce distractions in the child's bedroom (TV, radio, excessive number of toys).
- Model "how to" start on activities or tasks.

Structure a quiet place for the child to do homework.

- Adjust your expectations to the child's own pace.
- Have your child repeat to you the directions you give him so you know he understands what is expected of him.
- Set small intervals of work time for the child. Use a timer. Make chores a game.
- Let the child choose activities from two specific options.
- Keep the line of communication open with your doctor or pediatrician. Check to see if medication is necessary. Discuss school-related problems and any relevant observations made by school professionals about your child's behavior.
- Because some children are sensitive to certain foods, ingredients, or additives, monitor diet and sugar intake if necessary.

Although many factors contribute to ADD according to studies done by the Neurology Learning and Behavior Center in Utah,[4] one fact remains perfectly clear: These kids *can* learn. They want to learn, but they just aren't making it. We need to work together to unravel the puzzle. With a lot of hard work, faith in themselves, and patience from us, these kids *will* learn.

---

4. Goldstein, S., Ph.D., and Goldstein, M., M.D., *A Parent's Guide to Attention Deficit Disorder in Children. Hyperactivity*, Salt Lake City, Utah: Neurological, Learning, and Behavior Center, 1968.

CHAPTER 11

Passive Behavior

Eddie is in the 6th grade. He has been in LD classes for at least four years. He rarely brings his homework back to school. In fact, he tells his parents that he *has* no homework. Sometimes he does his math right; sometimes it is all wrong. When he is questioned about his inconsistency, he does not respond. Eddie's teachers and parents are greatly disturbed by his behavior because they don't understand him. Eddie refuses to give out any insights or information into why he does things the way he does.

For many people, the use of words is a magical and efficient tool used to express themselves, gain information, and make changes. For the learning disabled child, understanding what is said or written can be a never-ending stress from which he may wish to escape. The transmittal of thoughts is so complex that the process can break down in several ways. A child with learning disabilities may say or think, "I don't remember what she said," "She talks too fast," or "I don't understand what she meant."

Throughout the life of a learning disabled child, as communications become more abstract, the stress and confusion build. The parents may misinterpret the child's passive behavior, thinking that he can understand and remember what's going on. More often, however, the child's passive behavior may be an indicator of the difficulty the child is experiencing. In the example above, Eddie has chosen passive behaviors in his interactions with his parents and teachers. His attempts to cope, a conscious decision to not participate, is an attention-getting, controlled behavior pattern.

Passive behavior may be characterized by:
- Not answering questions
- Avoiding eye contact
- Turning away
- Refusing to try
- Agreeing to demands with no intention of following through
- Avoiding conversation, activities, chores, participation, etc.
- Not displaying emotions

A passive child may avoid conversation, activities, chores, or participation.

The learning disabled child may behave passively for a number of reasons:

- Acting passively may give him a sense of *power* since it can cause others to become upset.
- Habit; assuming he will not communicate well (negative self-expectations).
- Fear of invoking anger, criticism, or disapproval.
- Being sight or action oriented rather than verbal.
- Weakness in language skills.

A passive LD child is seldom a behavior problem. But he rarely does what he is supposed to do and seems to disconnect from the people around him. With his lack of performance and lack of responsiveness, parents and teachers become more and more frustrated, often displaying more emotions than the student.

We recognize that parents can be frustrated by passive behavior. Remember when you said:

   . . . "I don't know what he's thinking."
   . . . "He never does what he says he's going to do."
   . . . "Can't he do just *one* thing I tell him?"
   . . . "He only does what he wants to do."
   . . . "Why doesn't he tell me about what's going on inside of him?"
   . . . "I don't know my own son."
   . . . "She's like a stranger in the house."

Feeling "close" to the passive child is difficult because he doesn't or can't tell you what he is like, or why he is like he is. It is best to approach the child's passivity as a behavior that is the most comfortable for him due to lack of experience and/or skills. It is *not* a behavior the child is using to punish others. Parents with skills and options in communication can help their children to interact positively in the following ways:

Remediation for the Passive Behavior Child:

- Avoid criticism and be encouraging of *any* response.
- Encourage eye contact.
- Don't ask complicated or general questions. Instead of saying, "How was your day?" ask, "Who did you eat lunch with?" or "What did you get on the history test?"
- Use clear, simple, and concise words.
- Use puppets, drawings, dolls, or toys to act out conversation.

Use puppets, drawings, dolls, or toys to act out conversation.

- Build self-esteem and ego with smiles, pats on the back, compliments.
- Don't lecture, bribe, or punish for lack of response.
- Choose a few chores, be specific about what is to be done and write them down.
- Physically model chores around the house.
- Verbally model appropriate responses to questions and instructions.
- Practice conversations for a short period of time each day.
- Write down important things for your child to remember and *encourage him to do the same.*
- Talk with your child about what he is interested in even if you hate football and can't stand rock and roll.
- When possible, have your child repeat your instructions in his own words so you know he understands. Praise the child's physical and verbal responses.
- Be patient. Remember, your child is not you, he does not have your experience and he may very well have a different learning style.

Avoid becoming frustrated. If you feel your emotions start to rise, remove yourself from your child's presence for a while. Come back later with the same simple request or write down instructions for him to follow.

Due to poor communication skills, your child may be stressed when put under pressure to talk or respond. This reaction is probably not deliberate disobedience, but simply an indication of a need for a better understanding of what you expect.

CHAPTER 12

Aggressive Behavior

Irene just entered Junior High. Patterns from Elementary School are continuing. In the classroom, she never raises her hand to ask or answer questions. She repeatedly breaks class rules by getting out of her seat without permission, talks out of turn, or challenges another student on the playground to a fight. Irene wants to be the center of attention. She thinks she and the teacher are the only two people in the room. Thus, there is no consideration for others.

Irene may or may not be aware of consequences for her behavior. Her aggression doesn't register; rules and consequences are of little importance. Nothing internal prohibits her from repeating negative behavior over and over again, particularly if it will get a reaction from her parents or teachers. If she hurts the feelings of others, she feels little, if any, remorse or guilt.

As adults, dealing with aggressive behavior can cause us to feel confused, worried, angry, and drained of our energy. In order to deal with aggressive behavior effectively we need to define the behavior and understand what triggers it. The learning disabled child *may* display aggressive behavior. Below are some possible characteristics.

- defensiveness
- being outspoken
- wanting to control
- lack of response to suggestions
- blaming
- lack of predictability
- over-reacting
- self-critical tendencies
- social adjustment problems

- whining and complaining
- little eye contact
- emotional outbursts
- rigidity
- extreme testing of limits
- easily upset
- being scared
- concerned with *now*
- bossy behavior

The above characteristics are merely the outward display or symptoms of anger. Anger is a temporary strong emotion that can bring forth change and growth. However, aggressive behavior, which results from anger and frustration, attempts to hurt a person or destroy property. It is not the child's anger that is unacceptable, but the resulting aggressive behavior. An angry child with learning disabilities does not realize that he has choices in the way he behaves, however, it is possible for the learning disabled child to feel anger without being aggressive.

Why is he acting aggressively? The child with learning disabilities faces daily frustration because he is often misunderstood by teachers, peers, and parents. He may be misunderstood because of his:

- Difficulty understanding what is expected
- Inability to communicate effectively
- Poor memory skills
- Inability to grasp the whole picture
- Inability to make decisions
- Limited experience, awareness, and vocabulary

For the learning disabled child, the negative expression of anger becomes a catchall reaction to painful feelings associated with failure and low self-esteem, or feelings of isolation, anxiety, and sadness.

At an early age the child compares himself to others and often becomes envious when he does not receive the same praise and attention for his efforts. Angry outbursts may become a good disguise; the resulting aggressive act draws attention away from the fact that he does not understand what is expected or cannot do what is asked. Learning becomes increasingly difficult when disabilities are compounded with severe and frequent acts of aggression.

What are major accomplishments to the learning disabled child may seem like partial success to parents and teachers. A youngster may remember to make his bed and pick up things because it is important to him. However, he may forget to bring home his homework. A teenager may come prepared to class and keep his notebook organized but forget to clean the garage even after being told several times to do so. If the adult response is negative, focusing on what was forgotten, the child may come to believe that what he *does* achieve is insignificant, compared to the accomplishments of peers. He is angry with himself for not doing better, even though he tries. Lacking attention for what he *can* achieve academically or socially, he seeks to be noticed for his acting-out behavior which evokes a response from parents and teachers. When confronted, the child may say, "Who, me? I didn't do that."

The angry children we have encountered believe that other people's language and behavior must be directly related to their actions. They feel that they are the source of the teacher's bad mood or headache. They take

Bossiness and a desire to control are typical in the aggressive behavior child.

it personally when the teacher tells the class that they are too noisy or when the principal tells the students that they must try harder on tests. Since, for the most part, they are already performing to *their* maximum effort, they often feel guilty and self-critical ("I'm just not good enough!"). Sometimes these critical feelings flash into anger ("I'm doing my best!" "I *am* being quiet!").

These feelings may erupt in aggressive outbursts that disrupt the class and disturb others. At home, you can help by accepting your child's feelings of anger without allowing him to be abusive. Assist him in finding new ways to express anger more appropriately. Here are some suggestions:

Remediations:

- Teach self-talk: Give him choice words or phrases that he can repeat to himself when caught in difficult situations, such as, "I am doing my best," or, "I am okay. I just need a time out (or some space)."
- Set a few concise rules with appropriate consequences.
- Let your child know when he has done something wrong, but focus your attention on times when he behaves well.
- Separate the way you feel about your child from the way you feel about his behavior: "I can see that you are angry." "I feel mad when you break that rule."
- Give him choices of how to solve problems and discuss the consequences of his actions.
- Become aware that changes in routine and environment can set off reactions. Calm fears, especially when the regular routine is changed. Also, help the child anticipate change.
- Use closeness and touching to calm angry outbursts, if your child will permit touch.
- Model appropriate behavior. Share your own experiences about how you cope with difficult situations.
- Get your child to talk about what's bothering him. Go slow; be patient.
- Explore physical outlets like sports, clubs, youth groups, and scouting.
- Give your child an opportunity to teach others what he knows.
- Find time to spend and interact with your child every day.
- Rather than assume that your child will become aware of alternatives on his own, teach him how to overcome anger.

Become aware that changes in routine and environment can set off reactions.

- Give responsibilities in the home at which your child can succeed.
- Modify requests and demands so that he can cope and achieve success.
- Offer praise even for small accomplishments.
- Use repetition of rules or ideas you feel are important.
- Avoid verbal confrontations by writing down rules, instructions, or important phrases to remember.
- Try to stay calm.

Your child may feel safe and accepted enough at home to try out new behaviors to test the limits of what is appropriate. However, if your child is displaying aggressive, passive, or deficit disorders at home, then he is probably displaying some of those behaviors at school. These patterns will interfere with his ability to learn. In taking steps to remediate, you will ensure future success, particularly if you utilize outside available resources like counselors, therapists, or physicians who are available should you need them.

CHAPTER 13

Support Systems For Parents

We can't emphasize enough how important it is that you take care of yourself. With all the responsibilities you have, it is understandable that you could forget about the freedoms you have as a parent of a learning disabled child. So, in closing, may we suggest:

- That within the structured environment you help to create for your child, you love, enjoy, and support him. Continue to offer choices within limits in helping him to grow.
- Acknowledge to yourself and to others that your needs and opinions are important. When talking to professionals about your child, make sure you're heard; you are an important member of the team.
- Be aware that it's okay to be angry, impatient, discouraged, or sad with the LD child. Quit feeling guilty about having such emotions.

- Take time to be good to yourself! Go shopping, have lunch with a friend, see a movie, go to a ball game—whatever interests you.
- Take some time to be alone—to take a walk, or smell the flowers. Or feel free to spend a night out with the "fellas" (or "gals").
- Keep busy with activities and hobbies that interest *you*!
- Take a vacation without your LD child. Quit feeling guilty that you're leaving him or her behind for a short period of time.
- Commend yourself for wanting to learn more about your LD child, even if you feel like you're moving at a slow pace.
- Give yourself credit for having good ideas and being successful with your attempts at helping.
- Enjoy life to the fullest or the best you know how.

GLOSSARY

Special Education terms parents may hear in discussing their child:

Aphasia: Inability to understand or use vocabulary for communication. Experts believe it may be associated with an injury or abnormality of the speech center of the brain.

Assessment Plan: Series (battery) of tests given to determine if a learning disability exists.

Chronological Age: The actual age of the child in years.

Directionality: The ability to distinguish right/left, up/down, etc.—all directions from within oneself and the translation of those concepts to the outside world.

Dyscalculia: A neurological problem which contributes to the inability to do simple mathematical functions, i.e., calculation.

Dysgraphia: A neurological problem which contributes to poor motor movement associated with handwriting.

Dyslexia: A neurological or genetic problem that causes difficulty in sequencing letters in reading.

Educational Intervention: Any specific remediation which enables a student to learn better in the classroom setting. This remediation can be imparted by the classroom teacher or aide, resource teacher or resource aide, any Special Education or administrative personnel.

Impulsivity: Acting suddenly without regard for the consequences.

Individual Educational Plan (I.E.P.): Individual goals and objectives written by the child study team to meet the educational needs of the LD child.

Learning Potential: Child's learning ability as indicated by tests given by Special Educators versus actual performance on academics in the classroom.

Learning Strengths / Learning Weaknesses: Ways of learning which involve all senses: hearing (auditory), seeing (visual), touch (kinesthetic).

Least Restrictive Environment: An academic setting in which the child receives the best education, based on the child's individual needs.

Mental Age: Mental age level as indicated by testing.

REFERENCES

The following references expand on theories, diagnosing, remediation, teaching strategies, clinical information/case studies and overall generalization and information on the learning disabled child.

Bramson, Robert M., *Coping with Difficult People in Business and in Life*, New York: Ballantine Books, 1984.

Code, Marjorie, *Cues for Quicker Learning*, Sutter Creek, California: Essicc Company, 1971.

Delacato, C.H., *Neurological Organization and Reading*, Springfield, Illinois: Charles C. Thomas, 1966.

Faas, Larry, *Learning Disabilities: A Competency Based Approach*, Boston, Massachusetts: Houghton Mifflin Company, 1981.

Feingold, Ben F., *Why Your Child is Hyperactive*, New York: Random House, 1975.

Gearheart, Bill R., *Learning Disabilities: Educational Strategies* (fourth edition), Columbus, Ohio: Merrill Publishing Company, 1985.

Goldstein, Sam, Ph.D. and Goldstein, Michael, M.D., *A Parent's Guide to Attention Deficit Disorders in Children. Hyperactivity.*, Salt Lake City, Utah: Neurological, Learning, and Behavior Center, 1986.

Gordon, Sol, Dr., *Living Fully* (Bill of Rights for Parents), New York: The John Day Company, n.d.

Keirsey, David and Bates, Marilyn, *Please Understand Me. Character and Temperament Types*, Del Mar, California: Prometheus Nemesis, 1978.

Krumboltz, John D. and Krumboltz, Helen, *Changing Children's Behavior*, Englewood Cliffs, New Jersey: Prentice Hall Inc., 1972.

Lerner, Janet W., *Learning Disabilities: Theories, Diagnosis, and Strategies*, Boston, Massachusetts: Houghton Mifflin Company, 1985.

National Advisory Committee on Handicapped Children, *Special Education for Handicapped Children*, First Annual Report, Washington, D.C., U.S. Department of Health, Education, and Welfare, January 31, 1968.

Osman, Betty B., *Learning Disabilities: A Family Affair*, Consumers Union, Mount Vernon, New York: Random House, 1979.

Vale, Priscilla L., *Smart Kids with School Problems—Things to Know—Ways to Help*, Rosemont, New Jersey: Programs/Education Inc., n.d.

Wallace, Gerald and McLoughlin, James, *Learning Disabilities: Concepts and Characteristics*, Columbus, Ohio: Charles E. Merrill Publishing Company, 1975.

Where To Write For More Information:

- Parents Helping Parents
  535 Race Street, Suite 220
  San Jose, CA 95126

- Association for Children with Learning Disabilities (ACLD)
  5225 Grace Street
  Pittsburgh, PA 15236

- Closer Look
  1201 16th Street, Northwest
  Washington, D.C. 20036

- Orton Society
  8415 Bellona Lane
  Towson, MD 21204

- Foundation for Children with Learning Disabilities (FCLD)
  99 Park Avenue
  New York, NY 10016

- Council for Exceptional Children
  1920 Association Drive
  Reston, VA 22091

Journals/Periodicals:

- Academic Therapy Publications
  1539 Fourth Street
  San Rafael, CA 94901
- Journal of Learning Disabilities
  101 East Ontario
  Chicago, IL 60611
- The Exceptional Parent
  P.O. Box 101
  Boston, MA 02117

ABOUT THE AUTHORS

Mary Ann Dockstader presently holds a Masters Degree and a Standard Secondary Teaching Credential from the State University of New York at Binghamton, and a credential in Learning Disabilities from San Jose State University, San Jose, California.

Since 1975 Mary Ann has been actively teaching in the Special Education field, as Administrative Disability Diagnostician, Learning Disabilities Teacher, and presently as a Resource Specialist in the Oak Grove School System in San Jose, California. In 1983 Mary Ann was nominated as an Outstanding Young Woman of America in recognition of outstanding ability, accomplishments, and service to the community.

Laurene Payne graduated from San Jose State University and received a credential titled Resource Specialist. She has worked as a diagnostician to identify those children with learning handicaps and as a private tutor with school age individuals.

Laurene has worked in public and private schools with learning disabled individuals ranging in age from 5 to 19 years old. Since 1980 she has worked as a Resource Specialist Teacher in the Oak Grove School District in San Jose, California.

WHY CAN'T ANYONE HEAR ME?
by Monte Elchoness, Ph.D.

A guide for surviving adolescence written for teens and parents. Focuses on substituting hope, positive action, and communication for frustration, anger, and blame, with ideas for strengthening relationships.

$10.95

"PADS" ON THE BACK
by Jane Bluestein, Ph.D. and Lynn Collins, M.A.

Each set of "Pads" contains 96 sheets in 4 rainbow-bright colors to inspire recognition and positive communication in any relationship.

Eight different starters, including:
- A special thank you for...
- One of the nicest things about you is...
- It's nice to know I can count on you for...
- You should feel very proud of yourself for...

$3.95

THE LEARNING TAPE
from Self-Dimensions

Computer-generated Baroque music to help aid relaxation, stimulate right-brain activity, and enhance your ability to learn. Provides an atmosphere for learning stress reduction appropriate for home or classroom.

90-minute cassette, $10.95

WHEN CHILDREN INVITE ABUSE
BY Svea J. Gold

Seven authors join to help parents and teachers of difficult children explore reasons for behavior. Normal development, allergies, toxic states, prior abuse, nutrition, genetics, etc. are discussed; also ideas for detection and prevention.

$9.95

JOB LIST
by Bonnie Sose

Six months' supply of weekly chore charts for parents to use with their children. Chores include clean room, complete homework, hang towel and washcloth after bathing, put dirty clothes in laundry, brush teeth, etc. Includes space for self-evaluation.

$4.95

KID'S WORK
from Sugar Sign Press

Six months' supply of weekly chore charts for the non-reader. Develop good work habits and responsibility that will last a lifetime. Includes dressing, brushing teeth, making the bed, picking up toys, and more.

$4.95

PARENTS IN A PRESSURE COOKER
by Jane Bluestein, Ph.D. and Lynn Collins, M.A.

IDEAS FOR PROMOTING RESPONSIBLE COOPERATION AND DECISION MAKING.
PARENTS IN A PRESSURE COOKER offers a variety of methods for encouraging and maintaining positive, cooperative behavior from children without powering, nagging, threats, or force. Topics address adult behaviors and attitudes likely to elicit responsible behavior such as taking the initiative, making decisions, anticipating outcomes, and self-control. Clear and concise, illustrated with cartoons and highlights, this book discusses needs, motivation, and consistency, and presents strategies for creating a ''win-win'' environment in which everyone's needs are addressed..

$9.95

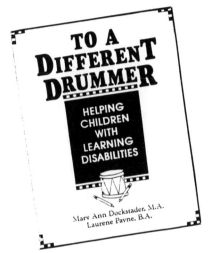

DO YOU KNOW SOMEONE WHO NEEDS THIS BOOK?

TO A DIFFERENT DRUMMER:
Helping Children with Learning Disabilities
by Mary Ann Dockstader, M.A. and Laurene Payne, B.A.

Great ideas for parents of learning disabled children.

$7.95